TFUD

(TALES FROM an UBER DRIVER)

By Gary Bruno

PREFACE

At age 51, I became a Deputy Sheriff. This followed a 27-year career as a banker. It has been the best decision I've ever made albeit a less profitable one. I did a little bit of part-time work as a limousine driver to help make up the difference, but didn't enjoy the "suit and tie" attire that I thought I had shed for good when I left banking. Shortly afterward, my son Jake became an Uber driver.

Jake pestered me on many occasions to let him refer me to Uber. His favorite line was "just sign up and do thirty rides and I'll make $300 for referring you. Then you can quit!" This went on for a couple of months. I drive a 2010 Toyota Prius which I keep in pristine condition. The last thing I wanted was for some drunk to vomit in it. I'm also a bit of a germaphobe so, aside from the physical mess, I'd be a mental basket case.

My limo driving was very inconsistent. I worked for a wonderful owner who would offer me rides that I was free to either take or turn down at my convenience. Due to my full-time job, and the uncertainty of when I would need to stay to work overtime, it wasn't always easy to fit the rides into my schedule. An unfortunate turn of events greatly reduced the number of rides I was offered. The limo company owner was in a terrible car accident. Thankfully, he survived, but was badly injured. While he was on the mend, he turned over the coordination of the company's trips to a senior driver of his while he worked his way back to normal. This driver had never met me and knew nothing about me, so I was hardly offered any rides. Something had to change!

I called Jake and told him I was ready to sign up as an Uber driver. Jake sent me the link to sign up and the technology immediately amazed me. While eating dinner. I uploaded my driver's license, vehicle registration, and insurance card into the Uber app. It couldn't have been any easier. The process of a motor vehicle background check and criminal history check was now underway, and I was about to get approved to make Jake $300.

By the time I left the restaurant, I had received notification that I was approved as an Uber driver. I opened the app, logged on, and started driving home. Within minutes, I received my first call, which I anxiously accepted. It was to pick up a woman at a deli...but I had no idea where I would be taking her. I picked her up, selected "Start Trip" on the app and suddenly saw the address of her destination. It was not a long trip, very uneventful, and I made about $5. I thought, "That was pretty easy. If I can get some longer trips, maybe I can make more than Jake will." I was still planning to quit after 30 trips, hoping that I could get them in before anyone vomits and then look for other part-time work. I did learn something very valuable on the first trip...as a driver, you have no idea where and how long each trip will be until the passenger is in your car and you start the trip. Very inconvenient but I saw the logic. Some riders are only going a very short distance. If drivers knew in advance that they would only be taking a one-mile or so trip, they may not accept the ride. The destination "mystery" helps to ensure that every Uber passenger gets a ride.

Although I didn't know it at the time, I was on my way to meeting a few very unusual, sometimes crazy, passengers. I hit 30 trips, Jake got paid, and I was having so much fun while making a good part-time income that I didn't want to quit. The addiction had taken hold! While the money is still nice, I feel like I drive more for the stories that I can share with my friends, which I've done on facebook over the past three years. At the time of this writing, I have completed 3,020 trips while earning a 4.99 driver rating. I suppose my passengers love me as much as I love writing the stories which they have provided to me.

I start each facebook Uber story with "TFUD". This serves two purposes...to alert my facebook friends that a potential side-splitting story is about to follow and to make it easier to search for every story at any time. Many friends have told me "You need to write a book!" So, why not? A word of caution. Some of the stories contain adult language and situations. I could have cleaned them up, but decided they add to the humor. There are a couple of serious stories thrown in as well. I hope you enjoy them!

SEX

TFUD: I had a pick-up in New Hope. It turned out to be two gay men going to The Raven. When going to The Raven from New Hope, for some reason, google maps takes you up the road behind the building for the drop off instead of the front. Knowing that, I wanted to make sure I dropped them off in front. Whenever I deviate from the map, I like to explain myself so that people don't think I'm trying to squeeze a few extra cents out of them. So, what did I say??? "This app always directs me to the back of the building; I'll take you to the front. You probably don't want to go in the back door." OOOPS!!!

TFUD: I'm having fun with the Raven comments now. Had another pickup in New Hope. Two gay men going to the Raven and, again, the app was directing me to the back...

Me: "This app always wants to take me to the back. I'll drop you off in front. I don't...."

Guys: "Oh, no, definitely take us to the front."

Me: " Yeah, I was gonna say, I really don't think the back door is meant to be an entrance."

TFUD: I picked up Tyrone as an Uber Pool rider. I immediately got a message "New Rider Added". I then stopped to pick up Rachel (a

2

young girl, maybe around 20, in Horsham at a restaurant in a shopping center that included an adult store.

Rachel seemed like a bit of a wild child and was talking some kind of nonsense while dropping F-bombs in her conversation with Tyrone.

Rachel: "Do you want one? I grabbed a fucking handful of them from Spice2nite (the adult store)."

Tyrone: "What's that?"

Rachel: "You don't know Spice2nite? Never mind then."

Rachel: (Seeing Tyrone looking at his phone) "You're looking it up, aren't you?"

Tyrone: (Chuckling) "Yeah, I got it."

Rachel: "Here, take one. They won't do anything to you, I've had about 20 of them. It's not like they're going to give you a boner or something!"

Rachel gets dropped off.

Me: "Well, that was interesting!"

Tyrone: "Yeah crazy!"

Me: "What was she trying to give you?"

Tyrone: "It was a Hershey Kiss, but I don't know if it had something in it or not"

Me: "Smart man!"

TFUD: I broke my arm the other day and am in a cast past my elbow. That didn't stop me from driving though. I picked up two married couples from The Raven last night. The women, at least, were very drunk. One husband got in the passenger seat. The other husband sat in the back directly behind him. The two women sat behind me and in the middle.

Woman: "What's your name?"

Me: "Gary"

Woman: "Gary, do you like tits or cocks?"

Me: (Laughing) "What???"

Woman: "You know, you picked us up from a gay bar. So, do you like tits or cocks?"

Me: "Tits!"

Woman: "Good, you're going to see some!"

I laughed as I started driving them home and the husband says "She's not kidding. She's showing you now."

Me: (Still laughing) "I can't see back there."

Her husband turns around and starts taking pictures with his phone. He then holds the phone in front of me and shows photos of both women with their shirts pulled completely up.

Husband: "I told you she wasn't kidding!"

Then I started hearing kissing noises and moans.

Husband: (Snapping more pictures) "Now they're making out."

He then shows me photos of the women making out with their bare chests against each other.

Woman: (Now talking in a 900-number voice and talking right into my ear) "Gary, are you coming home with us?" We only have two cocks and we need a third."

Me: "No, thanks, I'm happily married."

Woman: "She won't know!"

Me: (Nervously laughing) "Where the hell were you when I was single?"

Just then she and the other woman started reaching around the driver's seat and rubbing my chest...while the husbands are saying nothing! I'm driving with one hand on the wheel and the other arm in the cast and can't do a thing to stop them as they continue seductively whispering to me that they want me to join them when they get home. Then, the woman reaches around and starts rubbing my crotch and asking if I'm turned on. Luckily, I was way too nervous about the whole situation (between being married and having her husband sitting right next to me) to be turned on. I dropped them off and they remarked about how their kids seemed to be having a party inside. I suppose that ruined their swinger's plans anyway.

TFUD: I picked up a very drunk woman who, within about a minute, confessed to being headed to cheat on her boyfriend. The boyfriend "is the most amazing guy. I love him so much. I can see myself marrying him, but I need to do this". She then rambled on and on about her past boyfriends, occasionally calling herself "an asshole for what I'm about to do". Each time she said it, I tried to convince her to just go home (I hate cheaters!).

Woman: "Once, I found out my partner was a pill popper and I never even knew it the whole time."

Me: "A business partner?"

Woman: "No, my boyfriend."

Me: "So, what do you do for a living?"

Woman: "Oh, I run shit. I fucking run shit."

Me: (You mean into the ground...like your relationships?)

TFUD: I picked up a woman at the hospital.

Me: "Just getting out of work?"

Woman: "Oh no, I'm a patient."

Some small talk followed, and I learned she was from Ukraine. She then said something that I couldn't decipher but the last syllable sounded like "cock". Somewhat shocked, I looked in the rear-view mirror and noticed she was on the phone, talking in her native language.

Whew! Thought I was going to have to ask if one was just removed or just added. You never know these days!

TFUD: I picked up a woman dressed as a witch with fishnet stockings. Her perfume smelled nice. But then, along the way, I heard a wrapper opening. Then something smelled a little fishy, literally. When I dropped her off, she got out and was readjusting her stockings. I'm no mathematician but...never mind, I don't even want to know! LMAO

TFUD: I arrived at a house and out walked an 18-year old kid and a woman in a towel over a bathing suit. I was concerned because of a ride last summer when a girl in a wet towel soaked my seat, ending my driving for the night. I rolled down the window....

Me: "Are you wet?"

Woman: "What?"

Me: (now feeling like your average everyday Uber-driving pervert): "Do you have a wet bathing suit on?"

Woman: "Oh, I'm not getting in, just him"

Note to self: Never let your first question to a woman be "are you wet?".

🚗🚗🚗

TFUD: I just had back-to-back rides where a drunk woman used the word "vagina" multiple times. What are the odds???

🚗🚗🚗

TFUD: While listening to two couples having a conversation in the car, one girl who is a flight attendant is telling a story and says "I was deadheading..." The guy interrupts her and says "Wait, what is deadheading? Is that like a bad blow job?"

🚗🚗🚗

TFUD: I got called to pick up this guy in Doylestown last night. I arrived there and he was totally smashed. He got in the back seat and I started a 7-mile trip. Along the way, he was slurring to me that it's his birthday and he drank a lot. He was sitting directly behind me and occasionally patted my shoulder, saying "thank you".

Me: "No problem, I'm just glad you're not drinking and driving."

He kept thanking me about once per minute the entire way, each time patting my shoulder, sometimes leaving his hand there for a few seconds (which seemed like an eternity to me). I got about a mile from his home and he started rubbing the outside of my shoulder. It sounded like I heard "you're cute!"

Me: <Oh, shit!> "Excuse me?"

Him: "You're cute!"

Me: <DAMN, I thought that's what I heard!> "YEAH, that's what my wife tells me!"

I started speeding up, came up on a left turn and, as I turned, he flopped right across the back seat and I heard a thump.

Him: "OWWW, my fucking head!"

I turned around and he's face down on the back seat with his head on the rear passenger door arm rest.

Me" "Are you OK?"

Him: "You crushed my fucking head!"

Me: "Sorry about that, it was a sharp turn. OK, we're coming up on your house."

Him: (Sitting up) "No, this isn't my street."

Me: "Yep, this is it right here. Isn't that your house?"

Him: "Oh yeah, OK, (leaning forward) give me a kiss."

Me: "NO, NO, NO, I'm not into that! Happy Birthday, have a good night."

Him: "OK (leaning forward again), by the way, you would have liked the kiss."

YUCK!!! I couldn't drive away fast enough. I pulled over a block away and wiped Purell all over my arms.

TFUD: I picked up a young lady (YL) for about a 10-mile trip...

YL: "Can I request music?"

Me: "Sure, what would you like?"

YL: "98.9"

98.9 was playing a commercial

YL: " Do you have Bluetooth?"

Me: "Here's the cord. Plug your phone in."

YL: "Do you like Rihanna? I think she's so sexy."

Me: "Sure!"

YL: "This song makes me so fucking horny!"

One second of awkward silence followed that felt like 15 minutes.

YL: "I'm not hitting on you or anything. Just sayin'!"

<Don't worry...1) I'm married. 2) Mathematically, I could have been in your grandfather's class. 3) It's been so long since a comment like that was made to me, I forgot how to respond anyway.>

TFUD: I picked up a Mexican man (his ride request) and a drunk American woman from The Raven, on Cinco de Mayo, for a trip to her apartment. The man wanted to stop at Wawa. When he went inside, the woman started fumbling around with stuff inside her purse and said, "What the hell am I doing?"

Me: "What do you mean?"

Woman: "I just met this guy tonight. I don't know who he is. Now we're going to my apartment!"

Me: "So, don't go then. Tell him you changed your mind and I'll drop him off somewhere else."

Woman: "I don't know, I guess it's OK...but now I can't find my phone"

Me: "Are you able to locate it from your computer?"

Woman: "I think so."

The man came out and we drove to her apartment. They both got out to go inside and the man motions to me. I got out and he said "Stop the trip. I'm not paying for this. I'm not paying to find her phone."

Me: "That's fine but, if I stop the trip, I'll stop getting paid so I'm leaving."

Woman: "I'll pay for the trip, but I have to get money."

I stopped the trip and the three of us went into her apartment because I wasn't going to let their discussion inside keep me waiting. She got on her computer and found that her phone was at a restaurant she was at earlier in the evening. She got her ATM card and said, if we stop at Bank of America, I can get cash and give you $20 for the trip. So, we drove to the bank and she got out to go to the ATM.

Man: "She's drunk, she's crazy!"

Me: "Then you better not go with her. You know, you could get inside with her and start fooling around and she could cry 'rape'."

Man: "What's that?"

As I started trying to explain, he realized what I'm talking about and said, "if she does, I'll leave".

Me: "THAT will be a little late!"

He decided he's going to take the chance. We drove to the restaurant, it was closed, and I drove them back to her apartment and dropped them off. Now I'll have to claim $20 cash income for therapy services...for advice that neither one of them took!

TFUD: I got called for a pickup at Crossroads Tavern. It turned out to be four drunk women in very tight dresses.

Me: "How's everyone doing?"

Bride to be (BTB): "Great! We've been drinking all day for my bachelorette party and ended up here. Look at this video!"

She showed me a video of the start of the day where she's swinging a whiffle ball bat at a pinata in her tight white dress and misses and trips over a curb.

I started driving with BTB in the back seat with two other girls, and the future sister-in-law (SIL) in the passenger seat.

BTB: "Do you drive full time?"

Me: "No, mostly weekends. I'm a deputy sheriff full time"

BTB: (Unintelligible)

Me: "What did she say?"

SIL: "She wants you to put on your uniform and dance for us."

Me: (Laughing) "I don't have my uniform."

BTB: "Just take off your pants, then!"

We all laughed.

BTB: "I want to go see titties. I like titties. Who likes titties?"

Everyone answers that they like titties.

BTB: "Let's go to Creekside Cabaret (a local Gentlemen's Club)"

They all agreed except the SIL.

SIL: "I'm working tomorrow, I have to get home. Drop me off if you're going."

We dropped her off and the BTB says "I'm getting in front."

Assuming she's getting out of the back seat and getting in the front, I continued looking forward and suddenly noticed a right leg come over onto the front passenger seat. I turned to my right and found that I'm looking right up her short skirt as she's climbing over. <OK, this is going to be an interesting night!>

BTB: "I have to go to my house to get money!"

I drove to her house and waited in the driveway as she staggered toward the front steps. The screen door swung open with a male's arm holding it open as she entered. We waited a minute before she staggered back out to the car. She opened the passenger door with her shoulders slumped, head down, and a pout on her face.

BTB: "I can't go!"

Thank God! I felt as though I would have needed to go inside the club with them to protect them, considering how they were dressed and their drunken state. Not sure how I would have explained that to my wife!

TFUD: I got a call to pick up Mike at a local wedding venue. Mike came up to the car and said his wife would be here shortly. With that, Mrs. Mike came running toward the car, shoes in hand, holding her arms tightly to her chest due to what would later be identified as a likely wardrobe malfunction. I started the 20-mile trip and made some small talk (they were very drunk) but, within minutes, there was silence.

Sometimes, the destination address in the Uber app doesn't match the address in Google Maps, which I use for navigation. This was one of those times. The address Mike had entered in the Uber app was 3-digits and the one in google maps was 4-digits. What made matters worse, as I drove down their street, the house numbers would change from 3-digits to 4-digits and back to 3-digits again. How screwed up is that? I finally stopped in front of the house where it seemed to be directing me.

Me: "Is this your house, Mike?"

(Silence)

Me: "Mike?.....MIKE?"

(Silence)

I turned on the light and turned around to find both passed out cold! Mrs. Mike's dress was wide open, barely clinging to her shoulders. Her bra was completely exposed as were her legs. A belt was all that was holding the dress together AND Meatloaf was on the radio singing "Paradise by The Dashboard Light". <OK, this must be some kind of a joke!>

Me: "MIIIIKE???"

(Silence)

<Now what? If I get out and open the back door to nudge him awake, he may look at her and wonder if I had anything to do with her attire...or lack thereof>

I pulled into the end of a long driveway and looked back again. Same scenario. <Shit!>

Me: "MIKE? YO, MIKE???"

Mike: "Babe, wake up, we're home."

Me: "This is your house?"

Mrs. Mike: "Um, yes."

Me: "Are you sure? Because the app was giving me different addresses."

Mrs. Mike: "Yep, this is it."

I drove up the driveway and they both gathered up their things and exited.

Me: "Wait, don't forget your purse!"

After getting the purse, they stood in the driveway talking as I started backing out. Mike held up his finger to me and started walking toward my door. <Oh great, he's going to ask me why she's disheveled?>

Mike: "I think I left my phone in the car."

He checked the back and couldn't find it. I got out and checked with my flashlight. No phone!

Mrs. Mike used her phone to call him, but we heard nothing.

Mike: "Oh great! And, um, this isn't our house either, Babe."

Me: <WTF?> "OK, get in and show me where you live". We finally found their house and I dropped them off.

Me: "Have a good night...Happy Easter!"

You just can't make this stuff up!

TFUD: I picked up four young women from a visit with an older couple who owns a very large house.

Woman 1: "How do they even clean that house? Well, they don't have kids. But still, that would be too big of a house for me. MY house is too big for me!"

Woman 2: "But you need it for that nice big pool table.'

Woman 3: "Do you play pool?"

Woman 1: "No, I have sex on it!"

TFUD: Driving two middle-aged women, who had clearly gotten a head start at home, to a bar. They were laughing it up about one saying "motor boat". It was an inside joke but I couldn't help but laugh....

Woman: "What's your name again?"

Me: "Gary"

Woman: "So, Gary, I sent a picture of my tits to a guy, and he replies 'Incredible'. And she says to me 'I would have replied with a motor boat emoji' Haaaaaahaaaaa!"

What makes people tell me these things? LMAO

TFUD: Picked up four young women in New Hope. The one in the passenger seat says "I have a Prius too. Or, I mean a Priuth. Are you gay?"

Me: (cracking up) "Nooo, I just got it for the gas mileage" (checking our destination) "So, you're headed to The Raven? Speaking of gay."

Passenger: "Then I can tell you this story. When we bought our Priuth, the salesman asked my husband if he was gay."

As we pull up, there's a guy with an awkward walk heading for the front door.

Passenger: "He looks like he got some already!"

Other 3 girls: (laughing) "Oh my God! We're sorry!"

Me: (to passenger): "It's OK, I had the exact same thought. I just wasn't going to say it."

TFUD: Got called to pick up Ed at Cactus Grill. Old Ed got into the front passenger seat...

Ed: "Thanks for picking me up...I'm drunk!"

Me: "No problem!"

Ed: "If I stayed there any longer, I'd get in trouble. There were so many women in there and they're all looking for something....and they're all married! I can't do that though. I don't need that shit."

Me: "No, you don't want some angry husband looking for you."

Ed: "But, I'll tell you what...I just loooove pussy!"

Me: <Laughing>

Ed: "I do...I just loooove pussy!"

Me: <Still laughing> "Me too, Ed!"

Ed: "I mean, is there anything better than pussy?"

Me: <Still laughing> "Nothing I can think of, Ed."

Ed: "But I can't stay there or I'd get in trouble. But, man, I loooove pussy! I stirred up some shit in there though."

Me: "Uh-oh...what did you do?"

Ed: "Awwww, I mean dancing with 'em and shit. I was dancing with two, three of 'em."

Me: "At the same time?"

Ed: "Nooo, one at a time. God, I loooove pussy!" And I can still get it UP too!!!"

Me: <Laughing> "How old are you, Ed?"

Ed: "69...and I can still get it UP!"

Me: "Seems appropriate then!"

Ed: "Yeah, ha ha, man I loooove pussy!"

This went on and on for a 20-minute trip. I'd have to guess he said "pussy" no less than 40 times. And he probably reminded me five more times that he "can still get it UP!"

DRUGS

TFUD: I picked up a very talkative Alex at the train station....

Me: "Hi Alex....you're going to Lansdale?"

Alex: (loudly and excitedly) "Yep, I slept right through my stop and they said I could just get off here and wait. But it's coooold! So, did you celebrate the holiday?"

Me: "Ummmm, what holiday???"

Alex: "You know, April 20th?"

Me: (Oh Christ, I almost got through the day without hearing this shit) "Ohhhh, no, I don't smoke!"

Alex : "That's cool, that's cool!" (He then proceeds to sing along, loudly, to Magical Mystery Tour on the radio)

Me: "So you were in Philly for the night?"

Alex: "Yeah...you know how you meet up with an old friend and he turns out to be a piece of shit? It was like that. He was an old friend from college"

Me: <Oh, so I guess he grew up.>

Alex: "He just started talking trash about everyone and I was like 'I'm done with you'. He didn't like me either so it was unanimous."

Me: "Yeah, or mutual."

Alex: "He just wouldn't stop. You know, three strikes and you're out. Kind of like three strikes with the law."

Me: "Or baseball."

I think I'm done driving for the night. Not gonna push my luck!

TFUD: I picked up a young man and, a few minutes unto the trip, he said "Do you partake in cannabis?"

Me: "No!"

Guy: (after about 30 seconds): "I'm sorry, I shouldn't assume."

Me: "It's OK, I can't...I'm a deputy sheriff."

Guy (in a half nervous laugh and somewhat scared): "WELL...I'LL BE DAMNED!"

Me (laughing): "Yeah, good thing it was just some random question out of curiosity. Not like you actually have it."

TFUD: I picked up a very intoxicated couple in their 40s. About 5 minutes in, I heard the guy fumbling around his pockets and he finally whispered "Karen, I lost my weed!" She told him that's what he gets for leaving the house with it. The conversation continued while he searched until it got loud enough that it's obvious it's no longer a secret from me. Once he realized that, he says "Gary, do you smoke weed? I had this great shit...Girl Scout Cookie THC. It's fucking awesome!"

Me: (laughing) "Not for me, thanks. I'm a Deputy Sheriff. No worries since you don't have it, but you should probably be careful what you talk about in front of your Uber driver. You never know."

Him: "Oh fuck!"

TFUD: I picked up a crying woman.

Me: "Are you OK?"

Woman: "Just drive!"

Me: "OK"

Woman: "I'm sorry!"

Me: "No need to apologize". <But it could always be worse. My rider last night lost his 'Girl Scout Cookie THC' weed.>

TFUD: I picked up a woman who was extremely happy to be out (and way overly talkative) ....

Me: "How are you?"

Woman: "I'm fucking GREAT!"

Me: (laughing) "Why's that?"

Woman: "That was my father standing on the porch. I have 6 kids and he offered to watch them tonight. AND because you're not an Indian! I always get Indian drivers. The last one asked me where he can get weed. I'm thinking to myself 'well, I've got plenty. I'll sell it to you but I'm not going to just give it to you'. I gave him a low rating,"

Me: <I like my own rating right where it is so let's not tell this Chatty Cathy what I do for a living>

ROCK 'N ROLL

TFUD: I picked up this guy in the parking lot of a strip club to take him to another bar. He was a little strange and reminded me of Nicolas Cage.

Me: "How was the talent tonight?"

Nick: "Oh, I didn't go in."

(It was at this point that I knew I'd be writing about this ride, considering he's just hanging out in the parking lot of a strip club.)

Nick: "Hey, I just put in the trip to this other bar but, after that, can you take me to Quakertown?"

Me: "Sure, just change the destination on your app."

Nick: "Well, I don't know the address yet. I'm waiting for this girl to text it to me. Can I pay you cash upfront to start driving toward the Q-Mart? How much do you want?"

Me: "How about $10?"

Nick: "How about $20?"

<Hmmmmm, this is an odd negotiation. Maybe I should counter with $5 and see if he goes to $30>

So, I start driving to Quakertown after he won the negotiation and "Patience" by Guns N' Roses comes on the radio

Nick: "Oh, great song! Can you turn it up?"

Me: "Sure!"

Nick proceeds to sing the wrong lyrics to the song. Not the way people butcher the lyrics with what they think they hear...this guy is singing an entirely different song to the tune of "Patience"!

By this time, we have the girl's address and are almost there.

Nick: "Thanks for turning it up. I'm a singer/songwriter."

Me: (playing along) "Cool, anything I've heard?"

Nick: "No, but hopefully you'll hear me on the radio one day. Well, hopefully you'll hear me in your heart"

Me: <OOOO-kay then> "Well, it was nice meeting you."

Nick: "Do you have a card or something so I can call you for rides instead of using Uber?"

Me: <Oh shit> "Where do you live?"

Nick: "Perkasie"

Me: "Oh, I'm in Doylestown."

Nick: "Yeah, I guess that would be kind of far to start out."

<Thanks for making my excuse for me!>

Sometimes, people ask if these tales really happened. Folks, I can't make this shit up in my wildest dreams!

TFUD: Picked up two couples headed out for the night....

Me: "How ya doing?"

Guy: "I think you drove me before."

Me: "Oh yeah?"

Guy: " Yeah, I was going to a blues club and we were talking about blues on the way."

Me: "Well, if it was me, I didn't contribute much to the conversation because I don't know anything about the blues....unless we talked about anti-depression medication."

TFUD: Second to last pick up at 4am were two drunk guys. They wanted to listen to 90s music. One asked me if I thought Nsync or

Backstreet Boys are better.

Me: "They all sound the same to me."

Him: "What about Boyz II Men?"

Me: "I know of them but can't think of any of their songs."

The guy searches on his phone and then plays, AND SINGS, "I'll Make Love to You"!

I gotta start ending my nights earlier!

TFUD: While driving this young drunk guy home last night, he says "Do you have an aux cable in here?"

Me: "No, sorry"

Guy: "Damn, I wanted to play this song you and I would both like."

Me: "What's that?"

Guy: "Piano Man by Billy Joel."

<Huh???>

Now Gary is an Uber car driver
Whose Prius does not have a trunk
And he knows how to drive

To get me home alive
When I have set out to get drunk
Oh, la la la, di da da
La la, di da da da dum

TFUD: I picked up this mid-20s couple and the girl tells the guy in the front seat "plug in your iPhone to play your tunes".

Me: "It's not set up for that, but I've got Sirius. Feel free to put on what you want."

The guy searches and finds "Lay Down Sally". He shouts out "CLASSIC! CLASSIC!" and proceeds to close his eyes and play air guitar while mumbling all the wrong words. He gets to the title line and sings "WAY daaa saaa". He turns to me and says, "You know who this is, right?"

Me: "Yep, Eric Clapton. You know the name of the song, right?"

<crickets>

THE PUKERS

TFUD: I did some Sunday daytime driving. Figured it would be a relaxing change. Picked up Drew at the train station.

Me: "Hi...Drew?"

Drew: (getting in seated behind me) "Yep. Uuuuuuugh, please get me home!"

Me: "Rough night in Philly?"

Drew: "Yeah, my friend had a Halloween party."

As I'm just pulling out of the lot, I hear a burp and got a horrible feeling. Then, another burp accompanied by a slight gurgling sound. As I take a panicked look in the rear view mirror, I hear another gurgled burp and Drew's face looks like the one Chinese Brother who swallowed the sea.

Me: (for a millisecond, laughing at what it reminded me of, but freaking out) "Get Out! Quick!"

Drew jumps out and immediately throws up his Halloween party into the street. <Holy shit...I REALLY need to get started on my book!>

Oh, if you haven't read it before, find "The Five Chinese Brothers". I highly recommend it!

TFUD: I've got nothing. Developed a severe case of pukephobia at 1am so I went home.

TFUD: Had a pickup from a bar in Doylestown. The girl says, "We have a bunch of people and another car is coming so you can take these two (the drunkest girls in the bunch) and we'll catch the next one?" This is when I knew what I was in for and, like an idiot, I took them anyway.

I tried to make conversation but only received mumbled replies. With an 8-mile ride ahead, I watched every bump in the road and took every turn as if I had a bomb in the car. I got 2.5 miles from their destination and I heard a gurgled cough. I pulled right over and said "Are you OK? Do you need to get out?" No response. I asked again...no response. I started driving and I heard the dreaded sound of hell that I knew was coming. I was SO CLOSE to kicking them out right there, with no idea where they were or how they'd get home. Mr. Nice Guy held it in and drove them the rest of the way anyway. When we arrived, I finally let loose....

Me: "GET THE FUCK OUT! Do you realize how much money you cost me by puking in my fucking car!?

Rookie of the Year: "I didn't puke in your car. I puked on myself."

Me: "Oh NOW you're responsive!? Why didn't you get the fuck out when I asked if you needed to puke?"

Rookie of the Year (now out of the car): "I didn't puke in your car".

Me (pointing to every area with puke on it): "What the fuck is that, and that, and that? FUCK YOU!". I turned to what looked like the Birthday Girl, with a party hat on her head, who was still in the back seat and clueless. "Get the fuck out of my car right now! GET OUT! Happy Fucking Birthday!"

Wow, I had no idea I had this anger in me when I'm away from the softball field! Hope her friend enjoys the $150 cleaning fee she got charged. Fucking amateur!

TFUD: I got a call to pick up Danny. I arrived and Danny and another girl walked out flanking Danny's very drunk girlfriend. They opened the back door and his girlfriend flopped right across the seat, face-planting on the other side. As she tried to get up, I told her, and them, to not put her shoes on the seat. They sat her up and she said, "you're all assholes".

Me (looking for ANY reason to cancel the trip): "Who's an asshole!???"

Drunk: "They are!"

Me: "Good answer. Hop in, Danny. Don't let her puke or it'll cost $150. I just learned that last week."

POLITICS

TFUD: Sorry, there's no humor in this post...just an offer. The courthouse closed today so I decided to Uber. My first two rides were both to take people to drug treatment...one to Livengrin and the other to Aldie. In the few minutes I had with each, we had great conversations and I could tell that they are committed to their recovery (even not using the weather as an excuse to miss their therapy).

I felt very proud of them and decided I want to do something special. This Monday 2/18, on President's Day, I'm offering free rides to treatment. I'm doing this in honor of our current President who is trying harder than any of his predecessors to keep drugs out of America.

If you know of anyone in the Doylestown area committed to their recovery, have them send me a personal message and I'll get their rides to and from therapy set up. I'm only limiting this to my area so that I can keep the travel distance short in order to help the most people possible. If anyone has trouble messaging me, my cell number is also on my profile.#makeamericagreatagain

TFUD: I picked up a Spanish-speaking male (SSM). After exchanging pleasantries and hearing his accent, the following took place ...

Me: "Where are you from originally?"

SSM: "Guatemala"

Me: "How long have you been here?"

SSM: "12 years"

Me: "You like it here then?"

SSM: "Pretty much, yes. But Trump? No!"

Me: (Angel on my shoulder)-Gary, bite your tongue. Don't talk politics with riders. (Devil on my shoulder)-What??? Fuck him!!! Set this guy straight! (Angel)-Don't listen to him, Gary. Think about your 5-star rating. Don't risk it. <Polite laugh> "Hehehe"

SSM: "You know, because he hates Spanish speaking people"

Me: (Angel)-Your rating, Gary. Think about your rating. You've worked hard for this. (Devil)-Ahhhh...screw the rating, Dude! Tell him! Let him know that Trump loves him if he's here legally. Tell him how we don't want the illegals and the criminals here. Remind him he came here the right way. This is a two-vote swing! Take one away from the damned liberals and give it to Trump. Convert this bastard. You can do it! (Angel)-Gary, please don't let me down) <Another polite laugh> "Hehehe"

Me: "You're straight up ahead on the left?" (pun intended)

SSM: "Yes"

Me: "OK, have a good night!"

SSM: "You too!"

Me: "Make America Great Again!"

TFUD: I can see that this ride is going to test my patience....

TFUD: I don't like to talk politics when driving because it can impact tips and ratings, especially around Doylestown. I picked up this "slow" young man for his ride home from work today.

Man: "Did you hear about that school shooting this week?"

Me: <Uh oh, here we go> "Yes, it's very sad!"

Man: "Yeah, they said it was the same gun."

Me: <Playing dumb> "Same as what?"

Man: " The same as a lot of the other shootings."

Me: "Oh, you mean the same type of gun, an AR-15?"

Man: "Yep" <pause> "Because of the republicans."

Me: <Taking full advantage of the upcoming storm to drop an insult with a quick glance upward> "Ah, there's the first snowflake of the day!"

TFUD: I picked up a kid who was headed to work in Princeton. When I asked where he worked, he said he's working on an election campaign for (name I don't remember):

Me: "Good for you. Republican or Democrat?"

Kid: "Democrat"

Me: <Sorry to hear that> "Democrat" (because when I don't agree, I simply repeat what I hear)

A minute of silence is then followed by...

Kid: "But he's moderate, you know? "

Me: <Doesn't really make it better> "OK"

Kid: "Do you know Corey Booker?"

Me: <Thankfully, no. He's an asshole> "Well, not personally but I know of him"

Kid: "He's going to be there tonight."

Me: <Sorry to hear that> "Oh yeah?"

Kid: "My phone is dead. I hope someone can take a picture of me with him and send it to me."

Me: <Yeah, that and a token will get you a ride on the subway.> "I'm sure someone will"

As I pulled up to drop him off, a bunch of people were standing out front...no doubt, waiting for Booker. The kid gets out and everyone is standing there just staring at me. I'm thinking "Holy shit, how do they know I'm Republican!?" Then I realized "Wait, I'm driving a Prius. They don't think I'm Republican". Hmmmm, must have been the black eye and stitches I was sporting from my skin cancer surgery the other day. LMAO

TFUD: I picked up a man and three women who were all speaking Spanish to each other. The guy would occasionally speak English to me. I heard "Mexico" a few times, so I asked where they were from. He said "Mexico". A woman in back yelled "Mexico...and we LOVE Trump!" I pumped my first and said "Yeah, alright!" Turns out it was apparently Mexican sarcasm. Ooops!

LANGUAGE BARRIER

(SOME NATURAL, SOME BROUGHT ON BY ALCOHOL)

TFUD: I picked up Arnold and quickly learned he just moved here from Kenya in January....

Me: "Did you know English before you got here?"

Arnold: "No"

Me: "Wow, you speak very well. I can't imagine being able to carry on a conversation in another language after just 10 months."

Arnold: "How many languages do you speak?"

Me: "Just one"

Arnold: "English?"

Me: "Chinese!"

TFUD: I arrived to pick up an old lady at Tanner Bros. She had a few bags in a cart so I hopped out to help her. She must have been happy to see this American driver and immediately started rambling....

Lady: " I just got stood up for the 3rd time this week by an Uber driver. He couldn't find me, and he called me, and he was speaking Russian or something. I always get these drivers. They're either Russian or Indian or Pakistani or something. Why does Uber hire these people!???"

Me: (smiling and shaking my head) "No hablo ingles, Senora!"

TFUD: While driving a couple home, I got a request for the next ride. When I was close to dropping them off, the phone rang. I never answer the phone with riders in the car because that's rude, but I could see the call was likely from the next rider so I answered on Bluetooth.....

Me: "Hello"

Guy: "Shushepashie?"

Me: "Excuse me?"

Guy: "Shushepashie?"

Me: (long pause trying to figure it out) "I'm sorry. One more time?"

Guy: "Arumadria? Shushepashie?"

Me: (to my current riders) "Do you know what he's saying?"

Woman: "I just don't know, I was trying to help you out."

We were at their house so I said nothing at all to the guy on the phone and dropped them off. As I ended the trip, I could see that the next rider was named Walter.

Me: "Is this Walter?"

Walter: "Yeah, shushepashie?"

Me: (another long pause) "Walter, I think we have a bad connection. Can you say it one more time a little slower?"

Walter: "Should I shtep outshide?"

Me: "Not just yet, Walter. Looks like I'm about 5 minutes away. I'll be right there. Goodbye" <Holy Shit!>

On the way there, I figured out that "Arumadria?" was "Are you my driver?" So, I pull up and Walter gets in. As we start talking, I realize Walter has a speech impediment. OOOPS!! So, I spend the first few minutes of the ride telling him how it sounded like I've had bad connections all night long and I think it may be time for a new phone.

TFUD: I picked up an Asian couple who spoke to each other in their own language. They occasionally laughed. I waited until the next laugh, looked into the rear-view mirror, and chuckled out loud. They looked very surprised and didn't say much the rest of the way.

TFUD: I picked up three middle aged men. #1 sat in front and #2 & #3 in back....

#1: "We have three different drop-offs. How do we do that?"

Me: "After the first, just let me know the next address."

#3 immediately passes out on the leg of #2.

I stopped to drop off #1.

#1 to #2: "Give him your address."

#2: "I'll just tell him where to turn".

As we get near his home, #2 says "Just drop me off at the next intersection".

As I stop, #2 says to #3: "Brian, wake up. Tell him your address."

Brian sits up and tries to focus on me with his jaw dropped open, looking like R.P McMurphy right before Chief killed him. He, literally, can....not....speak!

Me to #2: "You need to give me his address."

#2: "Just drop him off 1/2 mile up this road."

So I drive 1/2 mile and stop at the intersection to tell R.P. to get out. He manages to open the door, staggers out, looks around, and just stands there wobbling. As I turned the car around, he's still staggering on the corner trying to figure out his next move. WTF is wrong with people that they get THAT shit-faced? And WTF kind of friend leaves his shit-faced friend to figure out his way home.

TFUD: I picked up a Chinese guy who was going to Philly. He spoke extremely broken English. He had just gotten out of work. I asked him what he does...

Guy: "Ah, chef, Ah, sushi chef. You drive pa-time?"

Me: "Yes, just part time. My full-time job is Deputy Sheriff."

He got so excited and said "Ah, you chef too???"

TFUD: I picked up an older family of four. One said that they're headed back to their motel. I plugged the name of the motel into

GPS and nothing came up. "It didn't come up. Do you have an address?"

Older Jewish lady: "Oh, youa not a very good Uba driva!"

<Actually, I'm the best Uba driva you'll eva have. What I'm not is a very good fuckin' mind reada!>

TFUD: I arrived at the pickup address and it was a hospital. I get a text that reads "I be where emergency at."

Great! So, I pull up to "where emergency at" and a pregnant girl comes out holding a child that looks like it was probably born the day she got pregnant with the next one. I asked her if she has a car seat and she said "No, I'm not going far, I can put a seatbelt on him." "I'm sorry, I can't let you do that." <That be endangering the welfare of a child where I'm at.> SMH

TFUD: I picked up Guadalupe and her daughter for a short trip. She got in the car cradling something wrapped up in a blanket. I was concerned it was a baby without a car seat...

Me: "What's in the blanket?"

Guadalupe: "A yeeneepeek."

Me: <feeling like Judge Chamberlain on My Cousin Vinny> "A what???"

Guadalupe: "A yeeneepeek!" (with that, a furry head popped out of the blanket)

At least I now know how to say "Guinea pig" in Spanish!

TFUD: I picked up two young girls (Candi and Sarah) in New Hope at around 2:30am. Candi gets in the passenger seat. Sarah gets in the back. Within a few minutes, Sarah is passed out on the back seat. I drive for about 5 minutes and make the first turn. Candi tilts her head to the left, toward my shoulder, looks up and says "Hallanuwallagu"

Me: "What?"

Candi: "Ha la nu wa la gu?"
Me: "I'm sorry...one more time?

Candi: "How do you know where to go?"

Me: "This cool thing called GPS."

Candi: "Where are you going?"

Me: "The address you put in."

Candi: "What address?"

Me: "xxx xxxxx Street"

Candi: "OK, good!"

I drive a few more minutes and she puts her hand on my forearm.

Candi: " I appreciate you!"

Me: <uh oh> "Well, thanks. And I appreciate you using Uber."

Next thing I know, she's out cold too but her hand is still on my arm. Then her thumb starts rubbing my forearm but she's still out. <Oh shit!>

I pull up in front of the house and shouted "OK, here we are!". Candi gets out and tries to wake up Sarah. No luck! I get out too. Sarah finally sits up, takes a few minutes then stumbles out of the car, almost knocking over Candi.

Me: "Do you need some help?"

Sarah nods, so I put Sarah's arm around my neck and we start walking her to the house. The porch light comes on and out walks mom.

Me: "Hi, I'm just the Uber driver!"

Mom: "Thank you so much!"

Whew!!!

TMI

TFUD: I picked up this guy named Steve around 11pm and he was waiting in front of the bar when I arrived (I always appreciate that). I started the trip and saw he was only going a mile. As I got close to his house....

Steve: "I'm heading back out in about 20 minutes."

Me: "Oh yeah?"

Steve: "Yeah, I just have to shit really bad!"

Me: <Waaaaaay TMI! But know I know why you were waiting for me> "Yeah, not something you want to do in a bar."

Steve (as he gets out): "Maybe I'll see you in a little while."

Me: <I sure hope not!>

I immediately got a call for a food pickup. I completed that trip and immediately got another call. I accepted the trip only to find out it was Steve at the address where I dropped him off. <Oh shit! Pun intended>

Steve (happily getting in): "Hey, long time no see!"

Me: <I really hope you wiped good and washed your hands!>

TFUD: I picked up three local college kids....

Me: "How're you guys doing?"

#1: "Good. How's your night going? Busy night?"

Me: "Yeah, it's been pretty steady."

#2: "Do you just drive part time?"

Me: "Yeah, mostly Friday and Saturday nights."

#1: "Do you mind me asking what you do full time?"

Me: "I'm a Deputy Sheriff."

#1, #2, #3: "Oh wow. Really? That's cool!"

#3: "I just had a not so good experience there."

Me: "Where...the courthouse?"

#3: "No, I was questioned by a detective. It was pretty bad."

Me (only half-jokingly): "Uh oh, we're you the one who asked the woman to kick you in the nuts?"

#1, #2: "What???"

Me: "You didn't hear about the guy who jumped out naked in front of a woman and asked her to kick him in the nuts?"

#3: "Yeah, I think that could have been me."

Me: "You THINK???"

#3: "Well, it was kind of crazy. I mean, they dropped the charges."

Me: "So that WAS you? You were the talk of facebook around here!"

#3: "Yeah, it was a really bad time. I was so stressed out about it, but they dropped the charges. I, like, had a breakdown in class."

Me: "What was it a prank? A dare?"

#3: "I don't know. I think she was just a girl with regrets."

Me: "So she made it all up?"

#3: "I don't know. I guess she might have."

I didn't have the heart to ask him "Wouldn't you know if you got naked and asked a girl to kick you in the nuts?" I think he's suffered enough!

TFUD: I picked up this guy at a restaurant. He hops in and puts his bag on the seat and I immediately smell onions.... I hope. It either smells really good or really bad. And it's a 9-mile trip so I really need to know....

Me: "Wow something smells good in that bag."

Guy: (one second pause.....which in itself scared the hell out of me) "Oh.....I work there. I had a sandwich, but I threw it out. I guess maybe the bag still stinks."

Me: <FUCK!...or not> "What kind of sandwich?"

He then starts to rattle off all the ingredients. I have no idea what he said but I noticed what he didn't say...."onions"! <Ewwwww!> It was at that point I think I threw up a little in my mouth.

TFUD: I picked up two drunk couples for a 35-minute ride. Different passengers asked me 4-5 times what my name is and how many kids I have. Both couples then took turns arguing.

The guy in rear right seat yells out "Who farted? That smells like a woman fart!"

Another argument breaks out between him and his wife. At the next light, he gets out, runs across the street and flips the bird as he runs away. We're now 8-miles from their home and one says "screw him.... drive!" And we left. LMAO

TFUD: I picked up a woman at Doylestown Hospital. After introductions....

Me: "Do you work here?"

Woman: "No, I've been very sick, and they were doing some tests. The doctor thought I had colitis, but it turns out it's just a bad virus."

Me (Thinking, of course): <Lovely....I'm just going to hold my breath for the next 5 miles. And it's such a nice night I think I'll roll the windows down. Would you like some Purell?>

JUST PLAIN WEIRD

TFUD: I picked up a guy who was going to Philadelphia...

Me: "Heading to Philly?"

Guy: <nothing>

Me: "How ya doing tonight?"

Guy: <nothing> <long pause> "Are you Uber?"

Me: "Well, I drive for Uber, yes."

Guy: "Are you 24 hours?"

Me: <OOOOOOKAY THEN! Yeah, I do nothing but drive, stop for gas, and eat all my meals in the car between rides. I've been going non-stop for over two years now and I could really use some sleep!>

TFUD: I picked up this guy from a bar just after 2am. He hops in, says he's only going two miles down the road and, I don't know what the hell he's on but, he proceeds to complain about his love life at about 100 mph....

Guy:"ManIdon'tknowwhatthehelliswrongwithmebutIcan'tgetagirl.

Icameherewiththisfatchickandshegotallcrazyonme.
What'swrongwithme?I'magoodlookingguy.
MaybeIgottagothechristianroute."

Me: "Yeah, Christian is the way to go."

Guy: "Yeahbuteveryonesaysthat'sgay. You'vebeenaround.
Don'tyouhaveanyadviceforayoungguytryingtodate?"

Me: "Christian is gay??? I'm 55 and I haven't dated in about 20
years. I don't think my advice would be fresh."

Guy: "Yeah,theysaythechristianthingisgay.
Theysay'howcanyoubewithonlyonegirl? That'sjustgay!'"

Me: "Hmmm, never heard that before." <Then it struck me. Holy
shit...what's that SMELL?! Dude, I know what the problem is. YOUR
FUCKING FEET STINK!>

I dropped him off, drove 20 minutes home at 23 degrees with all
four windows down, can't feel my ears, and my car STILL stinks!

TFUD: I pulled up to a house and out comes a guy holding a
backpack. He gets in the car and I see he's going to Doylestown
Hospital. He chats with me the whole way and, as we get to the
hospital, he then directs me to the ER entrance.

Me: "Do you work in the ER?"

Man: "No, I'm going to be a patient. I think I'm having a stroke."

W..... T.....F???

TFUD: H.S. Student: " Wow, the moon is so big tonight. I'm always amazed at how sometimes it's, like, almost not even there and other times it's just so big like this, like, how does that happen?"

< Dead Silence>

Me: "Soooo.... what high school do you go to?"

I have no doubt that I'll see her again one day asking the LQOTD (Lobby Question of The Day are funny questions I get from the public while working security detail in the courthouse lobby. LQOTD might just be my next book)

TFUD: I picked up two girls from a bar. One says she's having a bad night because her boyfriend is in the hospital. As it turns out, he was in a fight in the parking lot. Her friend proceeds to tell me the entire story all the way home. "He was, like, bleeding and shit from his head. He didn't want to go to the hospital, but I was like 'Dude, you need, like, at least three stitches. I'm certified in fucking wound healing and shit, like, I have a fucking certificate and I'm in grad school for it.'"

Dropped them off and wished her luck on getting her wound healing masters.

TFUD: I picked up this guy at an apartment complex at 1:45am. He never keyed in his destination address, so he said, "I changed it up, I'll just tell you where to go." I drove for six miles with him telling me to turn here and there. At one point, he told me to "take a left here"...but there was no left. I eventually got to a red light, looked across the street and said, "Isn't that the apartments where I picked you up?"

He said "Yes, turn left here!" so I turned and went about 1/4 mile before he had me pull into a 7-Eleven. He went in to buy a few things while I sat there scratching my head. When he got back in the car, I couldn't resist saying, "That was a pretty expensive trip to 7-Eleven. Why did we drive all around?"

He said, "Uhhh, I don't know." and made some weird chuckle sound.

Me: "OK, are you going back to the apartment now?"

"No" and he gives me an address 2 miles away, which just happens to be right down the street from a different 7-Eleven that we passed on our scenic route. HOOO-LEEE SHIT!

T-FUD: I picked up a woman who claimed to have been dropped off on the side of the road by police after a BAC test. She was DUI. Ooops....she should have called for me earlier!

TFUD: Ever been around a man who was wearing women's perfume? I just picked one up. It was bizarre...but he smelled pretty good. I'm still OK though, right??? I mean...it was only the scent I was attracted to. What's the protocol for that situation anyway? It can't possibly be "Dude, you smell really nice!"

TFUD: While at work, I got a radio call from another deputy asking me to phone him. He had a 65 y/o Vietnam Vet (VV) who needed me to drive him back to NJ. He had been in a NJ jail for a week on our bench warrant, was extradited to us, and released today. He didn't have the Uber app but had cash and would pay well. I also don't think he showered the whole time.

I made arrangements to meet him at 5pm after work. He was pretty interesting to listen to on the drive but he was sometimes hard to understand, was a little crazy, and had this loud laugh that always came in three bursts... "HA HA HAAAA!"

At one point, while he was telling me about Vietnam, he says "And then there was the IED. Here, give me your finger". He takes my right index finger in his hand, pulls off his cap and starts rubbing my index finger through his gray oily hair (Ewww EWWW!!!)

VV: "Feel that? Feel that?"

Me: (Trying to pull my finger off of his scalp as he keeps pushing down and rubbing his head with it)

VV: "Feel that? The IED blew my skull apart there."

Me: "Wow, yeah, I feel it. (I didn't feel shit. I just had to agree because my germaphobia was about to give me an anxiety attack if I didn't get my finger off his dirty head!)

Now I was frozen. I'm driving with just my left hand on the wheel and my right hand stuck in a ""We're #1!" position for the next 32 miles! (Gary, say calm. Do not touch your face, do not let that index finger touch your other fingers until you have the chance to Purell it and, for God's sake, do NOT, under ANY circumstances, touch your face or pick your nose!)

He went on with another story but started slurring a little.

VV: " Wait, I gotta fix my teeth. They took everything away from me and were supposed to take these too (pulling his dentures out of his mouth) but I kept 'em. HA HA HAAAA!"

Me: (OMG, now he's going to want to shake my hand when I drop him off. What the hell am I going to do?)

Sure enough, when I got him to his motel, he reached out for my hand. <AHHHHHH!> I "Purelled" it multiple times on the way back to PA but have a strong suspicion that I'll be snacking left-handed for the next few days until this is out of my head.

DEPUTY SHERIFF FUN

TFUD: Worlds Collide... I picked up two brothers going to Station Tap House. They wanted to stop at 7-Eleven for a pack of smokes. As I waited for them at 7-Eleven, I recognized a girl on the sidewalk who I had picked up from the hospital on Friday on a probation violation warrant. I shouted out "How are you feeling?" then explained how I knew her. She asked if I could give them a ride (she was with three guys). They were desperate so I said I couldn't because I was on an Uber ride but would come right back for them.

When I got back to 7-Eleven, I asked where they were going and I suddenly felt like Dorothy from the Wizard of Oz as I pointed to them one by one and said "I remember you from Bench Warrants today...and you were there...and you were there too!!!" So, I gave the four of them a ride to Horsham and lectured them, along the way, to stay clean. I just can't make this shit up!

TFUD: I picked up four very loud guys in their early 20s. When they saw a police car, they began yelling "Fuck da po-lice, Fuck da po-lice." I started laughing and one said "Haha, Gary's with us! Fuck da po-lice, right, Gary?"

Me: "Would this be a bad time to mention that I'm a sheriff?"

TFUD: While driving a drunk bartender home. The car next to us at a light takes off, cuts us off, and starts swerving all over the road, once even going up and down a curb. The bartender says, knowing what I do for a living, "Dude, if you want to follow him it's OK, just end my trip here and we'll go!" I started pursuit, called 911 and followed the car through Hatfield and into Lansdale while giving the dispatcher our locations. He barely missed a parked jeep, swerved left, and back to the right where he clipped a parked car. The police eventually found us and pulled him over. We sat there watching the guy fail his SFST miserably. My money is on a .30+ BAC. Love it when my two jobs merge!

TFUD: I arrived for a pickup location in a dark parking lot. Two Asian guys, dressed in black, with half-face skeleton headgear came out from the trees behind a house and approached my car. One came to my window and the other stood at the passenger side window. Of course, I'm thinking robbery. I was prepared and thought to myself "here's where your training finally pays off!" I cracked open the window a bit.

Guy: "How does this work?"

Me: "Did you order an Uber? Are you John?"

Guy: "Yes, but it's the first time I've used it and I don't know how it works."

Me <WHEW!>: Just hop in and I'll take you where you're going."

They turned out to be very nice, normal guys.

T-FUD: While driving a couple home, a drunk woman was in the passenger seat, and they wanted to stop at Wawa. I pulled in next to a parked police cruiser and she says "Great, you're putting me right next to a fucking cop!"

Me: "I've got news for you. You're already sitting next to one!" OOOPS!

MISCELLANEOUS

TFUD: Driving a drunk guy home from a local bar....

Drunk: "How's your night going?"

Me: "Not bad. A little slow, so I went home and watched TV for a while. Figured 11:00 was a good time to head back out."

Drunk: "What did you watch?"

Me: "20/20: Deadly Ride! It was about the Uber driver who killed people in between rides."

I got a $5 tip on a $5 ride. I'm brilliant!

TFUD: Pulled into a driveway but had to stop at the gate of a very long driveway. Waited a couple of minutes until I saw two high school aged girls running down the driveway. They were laughing and yelling "we're coming, don't leave!", and dressed like it was summer. They appeared to be drunk since it looked a little bit like a Special Olympics run. Girl #1 hopped over the fence. Girl #2 was climbing the fence with a solo cup in her hand. She fell from the top of the fence but, amazingly, didn't spill a drop. That's experience right there!

Me: "Are you OK?"

#2: "Yeah, I'm fine."

Me: "I'm sorry but you can't take a drink in the car."

#1: "It's just water. Show him."

#2: "Yeah, it's just water. You can smell it or take a sip."

Me: "No, I'm good. I'll take your word for it."

As they get in, #1 shouts "I'm so cold, I can't feel my asshole!"

I pondered that statement for quite a while before coming to the conclusion that my asshole is really not a part of my body that I'm keenly aware of whether I can actually feel it's presence, or not, at any given time.

TFUD: Got a call to pick up "Jane". Got there and Jane helped "Mary" into the car and said goodbye. <Uh-oh, this can't be good. Puker alert!> Luckily, she was only going a couple of miles. The race was on! <OK, keep her talking so nothing but words will come out>

Me: "How was your night?"

Mary: "Eh..I...guess...it...was...OK"

Me: "That doesn't sound good!"

Mary: "It's...not. I'm...bad...I'm...just...bad."

Me: <I don't even want to know>

Mary: "I...just...can't...wait...to...get...home...to...my...dogs."

Me: "What kids of dogs?"

Mary: "I...have...two...golden...retrievers. They're...my...life.
When...they're...happy...I'm...just...happy.
You...know,...even...if...they're...bad,...they...don't...piss...me...off.
And...when...they...talk...about...other...dogs...I...respect...their...
space."

Me: <They TALK about other dogs??? OK then, that's enough
conversation for me!> "Is this your house on the right?"

Mary: "Yep...OK...thank...you. I'll...just...tip...you...on...the...app."

Me: <No you won't, because Jane ordered the ride. But it's OK....not
puking in my car is enough of a tip for me> "Have a nice weekend!"

TFUD: Got a call to pick up "Mike" at NBI. Mike and his wife got in
the car seemingly pretty drunk.

Me: "How was the NBI tonight?"

Mike: "Ahhh, OK, I guess. We started out in Doylestown at
Hopscotch for 80's night. Do you know it?"

Me: "Oh yeah, in the Marketplace."

Mike: " Yeah, it used to be Doylestown Brewery, but they moved out. How is your weekend?"

Me: "My weekend? Pretty good. Just got back tonight from Connecticut, grabbed some dinner, and started driving."

Mike: "We started out in Doylestown at Hopscotch for 80's night. Do you know it?"

LOL, and THIS is why people Uber!

Note: I did think for a second about answering in the exact same way to see if we'd repeat the conversation but didn't have the heart.

TFUD: Took a little dinner break at McDonald's and the following drive-up experience took place....

Drive-up Kid: "Your total is $15.54. First window, please."

I handed him a $20 and he gives me back 46 cents and a $5, saying "I don't have any singles, so I gave you a five."

Me: (double-checking his math in my head) "Excuse me?"

Kid: "I don't have any singles, so I gave you a five."

Me: <OK, I don't think your manager would approve of your problem-solving skills, but it works for me.>

Then I pulled up to the second window and the next kid says to me, "I have a question for you if you don't mind".

Me: "What's that?"

Kid: "Did you ever brew coffee before?"

Me: "Not very often, why?"

Kid: "My manager never showed me how and this is what happened", as he held up an empty coffee pot with grounds caked all over the inside.

Me: "You need to use a filter!"

Kid: "Yeah, I did but I think it had a hole in it or something. I don't think I should serve coffee to customers like that."

Me: "No, I don't think they'd like it." <Try talking with the kid at the first window and see what he would do.>

TFUD (No Passenger Edition): Saw an SUV pull out way up in front of me and noticed the rear hatch was up. I figured they must have something sticking out the back but, as I got closer, I could see there wasn't. Then, a big box of snacks fell out and the snacks scattered all over the road. Suddenly, I realized that this woman must have no idea why 45-degree air is rushing through her vehicle. I sped up as we approached a stop sign and was planning to be close enough at the sign to honk and get her attention. She didn't even come close to a stop and made a left, rolling through the stop sign. That's when I decided not to tell her. Stupid is as stupid does.

TFUD: Picked up this know-it-all little weaselly voiced guy (LWVG) from Wendy's....

LWVG: "Can you turn up the heat? It's cold!"

Me: "Sure!"

LWVG: "OK, don't follow the map. I'm going to give you shortcuts."

Me: "Whatever way you want to go, just let me know."

LWVG: "OK, make a right at the next stop sign. You don't live around here, do you?"

Me: "I live two miles from here"

LWVG: "You don't know the shortcuts?"

Me: "Sure, but I follow the GPS so no riders think I'm intentionally going a longer way if I deviate from it. If they want to tell me something different, that's fine."

We get within a couple miles of his house and he turns on the back light and starts opening his bag to eat (Rude!...that always pisses me off). Then his window goes down. <hmm, now he's hot?>. Then it immediately goes back up <did he just throw a fucking pickle out my window???>

We turn on his street and he starts flicking the light on and off.

LWVG: "Which way is off on this switch?"

Me: "Just leave it in the middle"

LWVG: "There's no middle."

Me: " OK then, when the light goes off, just leave it in that position." <holy shit!>

LWVG: "There, that worked!"

Me: "My shortcut!"

TFUD: Picked up two drunk couples for a trip to Jersey. One couple was discussing their jobs and who was more important to the household...

Female 1: "I make a hunnndred ffffuckin' thousand dollarshhh a year!"
Female 2: "AND I PAID FOR FFFUCKIN' DRRRINKS TONIGHT!???"

TFUD: Got a call for a pickup. On the way there, the pickup location was updated. As I was approaching the street, I noticed a man on the corner, waiving me down. It was my rider, who had been drinking.....

Man: (jumping into the passenger seat) "How you doing tonight?"

Me: "Not as good as you!"

Man: "I'm just going up to the Creekside Inn."

Me: "OK. Where have you been tonight?"

Man: (pointing) "Right up here!"

Me: "At Skyline?"

Man: "No, at Creekside. My wife and I just took an Uber home, but

I'm not done. Sometimes you just want a couple more drinks, you know?"

Me: (laughing) "And your wife didn't mind you going back?"

Man: "I don't know. I snuck out the back door...HAHAHA!"

Me: (laughing hysterically) "Ahhhh, so that's why the location updated and you were standing on a corner" LMAO

TFUD: Picked up an older drunk couple around 2am. The woman opens the door, starts to get in and says "wait, do you brake for animals?"

Me: "To avoid hitting them, yes, but were not stopping to pick any up if that's what you mean."

TFUD: Waited 5 minutes for this guy to come out of his house. When he finally did, he walked out carrying about an 18-month-old boy like a football (and it's not as if he had something else in his hands). Then he gets in with the boy on his lap:

Me: "You don't have a car seat?"

Dickhead: "I'm just going to the train station" (3-4 miles away)

Me: "It's against the law to take him without a car seat."

Dickhead: "I'm just going to the train station."

Me: "I don't care if you're going to the end of the block. I'm not risking your boy's life."

Holy shit!

TFUD: Picked up a guy, probably in his late 20's. Driving along and seeing lightning (as I also did on the way to pick him up), the following conversation takes place:

Me: "I didn't think it was supposed to rain tonight but that lightning is getting closer and closer."

Guy: "It's actually just heat that is trapped in the atmosphere, blah blah blah blah blah" (as he goes through this long explanation of heat lightning)

We got a minute away from his house and it starts pouring rain.

Me: "Science class?"

TFUD: Got called for a pickup at 2:15am. Turned out it was for two girls and three guys (one more than my car will hold). As the girls argued with me that they wanted to squeeze five in, the happy drunk guys stood outside the car and broke into that stupid "Fly Eagles Fly" song. THAT sealed the deal! No way in hell were they getting into my car and subjecting me to that stupid song for the entire trip!

TFUD: After apparently being directed to the wrong address, I called.....

Me: "Are you at xxxx Point Pleasant Pike?"

Him: " No, we're on Preston Lane"

Me: "OK, this took me to the wrong address. What's the house number?"

Him: "No house number. We're outside."

Me: "Is there an intersection nearby?"

Him: "Yes!"

Me: (Holy crap) "OK, I'll just find you."

I pulled up, and they're standing directly in front of a house!

Me: "Do you work at Dunkin Donuts?"

Him: "No, why?"

Me: "Just curious. I ask all my customers."

TFUD:
Girl #1: "My father is going to take me deer hunting one day."

Girl #2: "How can you kill a deer!?"

#1: "It helps to control the population!"

#2: "There's, like. 4 billion fucking Asians in the world but no one is running around shooting them!"

Hmmmm, she has a point.

TFUD: Picked up a young lady from a large retirement community who reeked of onions.... or BO. I had to find out before puking at the thought of the latter.

Me: "Do you work here or were you visiting?" <please say work, please say work, please say work!>

Her: "I work here."

Me: "Cool. What do you do?" <please say cook please say cook, please say cook!>

Her: "I'm a cook."

Me; "That's awesome!"

Whew! I wonder if she was curious as to why I was so excited about that.

TFUD: Picked up rider #1 who says, "can we pick up my friend on the way and we'll throw you a few extra bucks for the trouble?"

Me: "No problem!"

Picked up rider #2 who immediately started bad mouthing the best man for the bachelor party they're going to because it starts with bowling.

#2: " I forgot my bottles of liquor. Can we go back?"

Me: "Sure!"

#2: (calls wife) "Babe, we're coming back. Can you run that red bag of liquor out to the car for me?" He then says to #1: "She'll do it. She's like a guy, but gives great BJ's!"

#2 (which is now a fitting term) then talks the entire way about the features and every piece of high-end furniture in his brand new house, who his neighbors are ("a bond trader, so we have that Wall Street thing in common" and "a pharmaceutical CFO"), his "new 911", and mentions they're putting his boat in the water in two weeks. He also suggested he thought the groom's "85-year-old millionaire grandfather should pick up the tab for tonight because he can't take it with him".

As we are approaching the drop-off, I hear #1 taking out money. Mr. Materialistic whispers to him "Put it away. You don't have to tip with these guys."

That final straw prompted me to say, as they exited, "Have a great time.....and you shouldn't talk like that about your wife!"

#1 reached in and tipped me anyway. He must have been glad I called out #2. Hahaha!

TFUD: Picked up a woman who had a rare night out away from her four kids, all under the age of five. She said " Yep they're 5, 3, 2, and the baby is 5 months. The 2-year-old is an asshole!"

LMAO.... I almost drove off the road!

TFUD: Picked up three young adults and their very drunk father who sat in the passenger seat. As we were leaving the parking lot, he turns to me and says, "Are you Italian?" I said "Yes, sir!" He slurs "I knew it because you have a nose like a fucking dago!" LOL... we had a good laugh while his kids were embarrassed as hell.

TFUD: Got called for a pickup on a one-way street. Pulled up in front of her place as far to the left as I possibly can next to parked cars and put my hazard lights on while waiting for her. A car pulled up behind me and sat there waiting to get through. Where I'm from, hazard lights mean I'm not moving until I turn them off. Having left plenty of room to pass on my right, I began waving him on and it takes him forever to finally get the message. The next vehicle that pulls up is a minivan and the Democrat (yes, they're easy to spot

because they have a certain look around here) behind the wheel
starts laying on his horn and waving his arm. I waved him on also,
but he kept up with the horn honking. I finally jumped out of the car
and yelled at him, "I can drive a fucking truck through there!". I get
back in the car and he pulls up next to me mouthing something. I
rolled down my window and yelled " you made it through, didn't
you, asshole? She (Clinton) lost...get over it!" With that, my ride
hops into the car. "Oh, hello. Sorry about the language"!"
LMAO #uberrage

TFUD: Picked up a couple in New Hope, headed to NJ...

Me: "How was your night?"

Man: "Ahhh, alright. She's mad at me because I fell asleep, so I'm a
dick."

Me: (laughing) "You fell asleep in a bar?"

Woman: "I know, right!???"

Me: (after driving no more than a block) "Wasn't it kind of loud in
there to fall asleep?"

(silence)

Woman: "He's asleep!"

Me: "Holy shit!"

TFUD: I pull up to The Buck in Feasterville to pick up "Ron". This guy in his 60s wearing a fur jacket walks up to the window and I say, "are you Ron?" He nods his head and staggers to the passenger side where he gets in the front seat. As I'm checking the destination, he mumbles an address. I said, "it says here you're going to Harrigan's Pub". At the same time, a couple walks out of the bar and gives me a confused look....

Me (to Furby): " What's your name?"

Furby: "Wayne"

.

Me (to Confused Guy): "Are you Ron?"

CG: "Yes!"

Me: "Great. you're in. Wayne, you're out!"

I later told the couple I've never been so happy to see them in all my life.

TFUD: Waiting outside Xfinity to pick up a friend and some drunk guy gets in the back seat. Not knowing how many were in the party, I asked "Are you with Pat?"

Drunk: "No, I'm going to the airport"."

Me: "Not in this car, I'm picking someone else up"."

Drunk: "OK, I guess I'll get out."

Me: "Yeah, that would be a good idea!"

TFUD: Picked up a guy who was pretty drunk and had a 45-minute ride to his destination. He really enjoyed talking about his many philosophies in life and talked my ear off the whole way. Each one included the idiom "at the end of the day". I usually worry that listening to such a habit for so long might rub off on me. It's all good though. The trip paid well, and he gave me a $10 tip but, at the end of the day, this job is all about relationships.

TFUD: Picked up three guys from a party. As we drove away, I said "how did you like the girl in the pink with the curves?". One guy says "Oh My God! Wait....how...???" I said, "I just picked up four other guys from here and they couldn't stop talking about her."

TFUD: Picked up a drunk couple from a wedding and the guy is talking my ear off the whole way about how "we're going to get engaged, I want her to be able to stay home and not work, I want to do everything for her instead of the other way around (then turns to her) 'Babe, you have my jacket?'" <Yeah....almost everything!>

TFUD: I get a request to pick up "Diarmaid" at an address last night. Pulled into the driveway and waited. Finally, this guy comes out wearing shorts and what looked like a pajama shirt and I'm thinking "where the hell is this guy going dressed like that?" Rolled down my window and he shouts, "can I help you?"

Me: "Diarmaid?"

PJ Man: "What?"

Me: (double checking my phone) "Are you Diarmaid?"

PJ Man: "Huh???"

Me: "I'm supposed to pick up someone named Diarmaid at this address."

PJ Man: "Well you have the wrong address"

Of course, this couldn't happen when I'm picking up a Joe or a Mary.

TFUD 3:30am I take a call from a guy in Hatfield. I pull up and it's three teenage girls, about age 13, I suppose, on a corner and a shirtless, maybe 15 y/o, boy. The three girls get in the car and the boy looks into my window and says, "get them home safely!"

Me: <Whaaaaat!???> "Yo, Biebs, I'm a grown man, I think I can handle that.! The only reason they're getting in my car is because I can't trust the next driver you call.

TFUD:
Young Male Passenger: "I thought about being an Uber driver."

Me: "Yeah?"

YMP: "Yeah, but I became an alcoholic instead."

T-FUD: As I dropped off a group last night and they took up a collection to tip me, the last one out turns around to give me a $20 and says, "Here's another Tubman!" LMAO!

TFUD: Got called to pick up Joe at Stephanie's in Doylestown. Prices were surging and I was going to get a $28 bonus for the ride...so there was no way I was going to let anyone screw it up. I pulled up, sat for about 30 seconds, and a very large (probably 300 lb.), very drunk girl got in the passenger seat.

Me: "What's your name?"

VLVDG: "Patty"

Me: "This isn't your ride. I'm picking up Joe?"

VLVDG: "111 xxxxxx Street"

Me: "This is Joe's ride".

VLVDG: "He left. He said I can take his Uber, 111 xxxxxx Street""

Me: "OK, I'll start the trip. If a different address comes up, you'll have to get out."

VLVDG: "111 xxxxxx Street" (she just kept repeating this)

Me: "This says 222 yyyyyy Street. Get out!"

We argued about this for another minute with me trying to explain that, if I take her to a different address, Joe can dispute it and I won't get paid. Then "Rider Cancelled" popped up on the app.

Me: "Joe just cancelled. Get out!"

VLVDG: "111 xxxxx Street"

Just then, I got another ride request from Chris, also at Stephanie's

Me: "Now I'm picking up Chris. Get out!"

VLVDG: " Well, he's not here! 111 xxxxxx Street."

Me: "See those three cops standing in front of my car? I'm about to get them to drag you out of here."

VLVDG: (getting out) "You're a fucking asshole!"

Me: "Yep, and you make the rockin' world go 'round!"

TFUD: Picked up a young couple in town. We stopped at the first light and the guy starts laughing and says "Check this guy out! He's

face timing." I looked and there was a Hispanic guy standing right next to us giving the finger to his phone and laughing. My passenger rolls down the window and I hear the Hispanic guy yelling "You should have come out! You should have come out!"

My passenger yells "Yo, turn it toward me!" The Hispanic guy turns the phone around and walks to the window. My passenger leans out, giving the finger to the phone, and starts yelling "You should have come out, bro!" On the screen was a very confused looking Hispanic male wondering who this guy is yelling at him.

TFUD: I picked up Steve for a 7-mile trip and recognized him from a prior trip...

Me: "How's it going? I think I've picked you up before."

Steve: "That's pretty likely. I Uber a LOT!"

Me: "Hey, when you add up the cost of a car, gas, maintenance, and insurance, you're probably better off."

Steve: "Not me! I did the math, and, in the last seven months, I've spent $4,500 on Uber."

Me: "Do you not have a car or not have a license?"

Steve: "I lost my license due to unpaid parking tickets. I had like 50 of them! But they add on a warrant fee for each one and a Constanoble fee for each one."

Me: <Constanoble??? I wonder if that's what they called Constables in Constantinople?>

Steve: "I tried getting them to reduce it so I can pay it off quicker, but they won't. Even if they just got rid of the Constanoble fee, it would help."

Me: <Yeah, because paying for all those fees PLUS Uber would be just about impossinoble!>

TFUD: I got called to pick up a very drunk Fred for a 2-mile trip. Fred stood with the car door open asking a female (possibly his wife) whether she's coming. She refused and Fred got in. I headed for the parking lot exit with the GPS telling me to take a right...

Fred: "Make a left. Don't listen to her!"

Me: "Are you sure? She's rarely wrong on short trips."

Fred: "Make a left. It's faster."

Me: "OK" (made the left) "Now she's telling me to go straight. Is that right?"

Fred: "No, make a right here."

I made the right.

Fred: "Where the hell are we?"

Me: "In the parking lot you told me to turn into. There's no way through."

Fred: "OK, just do what she says."

Me: <Maybe you want to follow your wife's advice in the future. Just a thought.>

TFUD: I picked up Karen and Mark for a 10-mile trip. We talked a little and they didn't seem too drunk, then things got quiet. After a couple minutes, I heard a lot of moving around in the back seat and the back of my arm kept getting bumped. I was starting to worry there was something sexual going on in the back. At one point, after getting bumped again, I took a quick glance to see what it was. I could tell that Karen was lying down, but I wasn't able to see why. Mark chuckled and said "She's just getting comfortable. Sorry!" I'm thinking.... that's what 'm afraid of!

We arrived at their house and Mark says "Karen, wake up. We're home." Karen was lying down, completely passed out. Mark tried getting her up from the driver's side but couldn't. He went around to the passenger side, where her head was, and I joined him. He opened the door but still couldn't wake her. He tried many times to drag her out by her arm but couldn't.

Finally, he was making some progress and I was able to grab the other arm. We stood her up, but she grabbed the door and wanted to get back in to sleep. We started walking her to the house with her practically asleep on her feet. Mark says, "C'mon Karen, you want to have wings when we get in?" Suddenly, she wakes up and says "Yes!" She turned to me and said "It's OK, Mark has me from here. You're adorable though."

LOL, yeah, I know!

TFUD: I was called to pick up Jim from a soccer club about four hours after the USA women won the World Cup...so I knew it could be a rough one. I pulled up and Jim started walking toward my car along with his friend, Dude. Jim called him Dude so much that I figured it must be his name.

They were both smashed and Dude walked partly sideways with his head bobbing and his mouth open. If "shit-faced" was in the dictionary along with a photo, it would be Dude's face.

Jim: "Dude, I only drank two beers today." Those shots were a killer though."

Me: "What kind of shots?"

Jim: "Zzzzscreaming Nachis! Zzzzscr, Zzzzscr, Zzzzscreaming Nazis!"

Me: "What's in that?"

Jim: "Rrrumple Minzzze and Jagermmmeister. Dude, weren't they strong?"

Dude was seated directly behind me and he couldn't speak.

A few minutes into the trip, Dude put his window down and stuck his head out. <Oh shit!> The next thing I heard was "ppppp". It's the sound one makes when they really don't spit, but it comes out and runs down their chin. Trust me, it's easy to tell from the sound that it didn't get far <Great, that's running down the side of my door now!> Dude then put his window back up.

A few minutes later, a hand shot up next to me, alongside my face. Dude sat up, close to my ear, but said nothing. <Now I know why he's called Dude because all I could think was "Dude, don't you dare puke on my shoulder and console or I'll throat-punch you!>

Dude stayed in this position for about half-mile, saying absolutely nothing. I kept looking in the mirror to see his shit-faced look, with his mouth hanging open. His head was bobbing like a 3-month old baby on his stomach, trying to hold his head up.

Jim: "I think he'sss gonna say something!"

Dude: (Finally speaking) "Hang a left up here!"

Me: "My GPS says I'm making a right."

Jim: "Dude, ssshut up. He knowsss where he's going! If he makesss a left, we're going away from your house."

I sweated out the final mile, hoping that projectile vomit wouldn't come my way. I dropped them off and Dude staggered out of the car. I pulled away, got out to check my car and, sure enough, Dude's spit was on the door. Who says I don't know spit!?

TFUD: I got a call to pick up Venus for a 54-minute trip.

Me: <Hmmm, Venus? 54-minute trip? Must be an exotic dancer who lives in the burbs and is headed to a Gentlemen's Club in Philly......She's got it. Yeah baby, she's got it. Well, I'm your Venus. I'm your fire. At your desire!>

I get closer to the pickup address and it's getting close to Peace Valley Park.

Me: <Wait a minute, this is AT Peace Valley Park. WTF???>

I pulled into the park and the pinned location is a pavilion where there is a party with a bunch of Indians. A fat Indian woman starts walking toward my car, followed by an old Indian woman. She then waives over a young Indian boy to come with them.

Me: <What? Where's Venus???> (Rolling down the window) "Hi, Venus?"

As the window went down, the breeze came in.

Me: <OMG, please, please, please tell me they served Italian hoagies at this party!>

Big Venus: "Yes"

Me: <Damn, thought so!>

They get in the car, with the boy in front and Big Venus and her mom in the back. I start driving the 54-minute trip to Philly (well, Philly is the only part of my assumption that was correct). Venus and her mom start talking Indian to each other.

Big Venus: "Daada dook a mula bala ba BURP daca bada..."

Me: <WTF? Did she just burp and not excuse herself????>

Big Venus : "Daada dook a mula bala ba BURRRRRP daca bada..."

Me: <Holy shit, that was DEFINITELY a burp! Excuse yourself and teach this kid some manners, will ya?>

There was no apology from Big Venus at all, She just continued talking and left me thinking <52 minutes to go! Maybe if I crash, I'll get airlifted out of this sub shop and somehow survive!>

IN ALL SERIOUSNESS

TFUD: Sorry, not a funny one. Just a PSA... Please educate your kids about ways to verify their driver. Picked up a young teen boy and his pre-teen sister at a Pub last night. Their mon "Linda" was inside waiting for their sister to get off from work. They hopped right into my car and asked, "Are you here for Linda?" while getting in. I had to explain along the way that was the wrong time to ask the wrong question. They should have asked, before getting in, "Who are you here for?" and made me say "Linda". Glad I was there to educate them instead of kidnap them.

TFUD: Got a call to pick up Lynn and immediately received a phone call...

Woman: "Hi, this is Lynn. You're not picking me up, you're picking up my son.

Me: "OK"

Woman: "Can you message me when you get there, and I'll tell him to come out?"

Me: "Sure!"

I messaged Lynn when I arrived. and a teenager came out from behind the house. He walked to the back of my car, stopped for a few seconds, then came to the driver's side. I rolled down the window.

Kid: "What's your name?"

Me: "Gary...is Lynn your Mom?"

Kid: "Yes" (and he got in the back seat)

Me: "Did you just take a picture of my license plate?"

Kid: "Yeah, my Mom makes me do that and send it to her."

Me: "Tell her I said she's a great Mom!"

Made in the
USA
Monee, IL